Code Billy
75 *Real Life*
Meditations

Jim Marshall

🕊 dustjacket

DEDICATION

"Code Billy" represents many years of living life and trying to learn from my experiences. Along the way I've had the privilege of knowing some of the finest people on earth. Each has influenced my life but none as much as my wonderful family: my loving wife, Marg, patiently ministering with me for nearly 40 years. My children, Hyperion, Landon, Saralyn and Jaime who have taught me much about our culture. My sister, Tammy and mother, Evelyn and my wife's family, who helped and supported us as we waited four and one-half years for a new church in which to minister.

To these and many more I dedicate these devotionals...may they bless others as I have been blessed!

--JIM MARSHALL

FOREWORD

Code Billy: 75 Real Life Mediations, has been written by someone who knows how to have a daily devotional life. My lifelong friend, Jim Marshall, has penned a classic treatise on the believers' walk with Christ. I've been privileged to travel on the road of life with Jim. This book allows me to take a spiritual journey with this good and godly man. I encourage all church leaders to use this book to grow closer with our Lord as well as to guide others to follow in the footsteps of our Savior. A must read for anyone who wants to drink deeply from the rivers of living water and grow as a spiritual leader.

-Dr. Stan Toler
Bestselling author
Oklahoma City, Oklahoma

.

1
"CODE BILLY"

After two weeks in ICU, two more weeks in the stroke ward, and seven weeks in rehab hospital, my daughter was released to go home. As last minute paperwork was being signed, an announcement came over the intercom saying, "Attention 2nd floor staff—Code Billy."

(A "Code Billy" — named after a patient who had spent many months in the hospital — was used to inform the staff that someone was getting to go home.)

One of the support people, who had assisted my daughter through her recovery days, now guided her wheelchair down the hall and onto the elevator with my wife, son and me in tow. As we rounded the corner on the 1st floor, ahead of us stood doctors, nurses and technicians lining the hallway applauding as we walked and rolled between them. Several were crying as our procession passed. It was a day of triumph for a patient who surpassed all their expectations. Mom and Dad joined in their tears of joy.

We go through life not knowing the future. Day by day we push ahead with our duties and schedules, trying to enjoy life to the fullest. When tragedy strikes and setbacks come, it makes us ask "Why?" We don't understand and can feel all alone.

But every once in a while, the curtain is pulled back and we get a glimpse of the love and support we do have. Family, friends, even strangers are lined up praying and pulling for us. It's a new day—we will walk again!

Hebrews 12: 1 (New International Version) Therefore, since we are surrounded by such a huge crowd of witnesses to the life of faith, let us strip off every weight that slows us down, especially the sin that so easily trips us up. And let us run with endurance the race God has set before us.

2
"BLACKOUT PERIOD"

During the early days of space exploration, millions of us were glued to our TV screens waiting for the capsule to be located somewhere in the ocean. Prior to splashdown we had to endure a time of Blackout in which there was no communication between controllers on the ground and the people in the spaceship. Reentering earth's atmosphere was very risky due to the extreme heat build-up on the space module. News commentators kept reminding us of the possibility of disaster and loss of life should the heat shields fail. So, we waited, hoping and praying that all would be well.

Blackout periods come to all of us during our lives. Whether it's not being able to contact a loved one or waiting to hear the doctor's diagnosis or hoping you'll get the job--we struggle with these times and hope for the best.

What do you do during these Blackout Periods? I don't have all the answers but here are some of the things I do:

I keep telling myself that most of my worries will never happen so relax.

I become more sensitive to God speaking to me through scripture, other people, things I read, like a billboard in my town which says TRUST GOD. Even in TV shows God often communicates His love for me.

Remembering how God has provided and cared for me and my family across many years comforts me that His answer is already on the way. I just have to wait which is not easy but doable.

The words of my wonderful mother give me strength as I wait in the dark: "This too shall pass." You may be in a Blackout Period right now. Take heart, be of good cheer! Rescue is close at hand. Let there be Light!

Psalm 91: 1-4 (New International Reader's Version)

The person who rests in the shadow of the Most High God
    will be kept safe by the Mighty One.
 I will say about the Lord,
    "He is my place of safety.
    He is like a fort to me.
    He is my God. I trust in him."
He will certainly save you from hidden traps
    and from deadly sickness.
He will cover you with his wings.
    Under the feathers of his wings you will find safety.
    He is faithful. He will keep you safe like a shield or a tower.

3
"ASSISTANCE NEEDED
AT THE MANGER SCENE"

A pastor was walking through a large department store one day when he heard the following announcement: "Your attention please! Assistance needed at the manger scene."

In this day of ridiculous political correctness, one has to commend the store owners for even having a manger scene. But, beyond that, all of us need assistance as we focus on the significance of what happened at the manger.
First, in our busy, stressed-filled world, it's quite easy to have no room in our thinking or schedule to personally worship Christ. We give gifts to others but too often neglect Him on his birthday.

Secondly, life throws us many challenges that can and will erode our faith if we allow. We need divine assistance to start at Bethlehem but not to stay there. Jesus grew up and became the savior of the world. We need to move past the sentiment of a baby to a vital relationship with our risen Lord.

Finally, don't forget there are many needy people desiring assistance at the manger scene. Most likely they are now more open and ready to believe and receive the greatest present of all—Christ Himself. We have the high privilege of assisting others in their faith journey by accepting and loving them unconditionally.

Luke 2: 12 There were sheepherders camping in the neighborhood. They had set night watches over their sheep. Suddenly, God's angel stood among them and God's glory blazed around them. They were terrified. The angel said, "Don't be afraid. I'm here to announce a great and joyful event that is meant for everybody, worldwide: A Savior has just been born in David's town, a Savior who is Messiah and Master. This is what you're to look for: a baby wrapped in a blanket and lying in a manger." (The Message)

4
"GIVE THE WORLD A SMILE"

Riding elevators can be quite interesting. Visiting family and friends, I have shared the up-and-down journey with various types of people. On one ride I encountered a hospital employee, and after we exchanged our obligatory greetings, he said, "My life goes better when I smile my way through the day."

It takes real effort to smile, especially when we don't feel like it, which, for some, may be most of the time. Smiling defeats negative thinking, lifts our spirit and makes us more attractive. Others are drawn to us because of our positive energy. We may even change someone's life by a simple smile at the right time.

When I think about the heroes - influences in my life - they all have a smile that assures me "things are gonna be alright." No words have to be spoken—just their confident countenances help me to forget about myself and focus on the good things in life.

There's a song that says, "You're the only Jesus some will ever see." If this be true, why not let others see HIM smiling at them?

Proverbs 15:13 A cheerful heart brings a smile to your face; a sad heart makes it hard to get through the day. (The Message)

5
OUR # 1 JOB

A long time ago I learned that it's very important to make our boss look good. To do so requires intentionality and consistency. When we reflect positively on the one above us everybody wins.

As Christians our # 1 responsibility is to bring glory to God. Making Him look good is more necessary than ever. Never in my lifetime have I've seen so much derision and outright disrespect for deity. Jesus, in particular, is too often joked about and belittled. God the Father is habitually referred to as OMG when people are surprised or upset.

So, how do we elevate the Trinity in our world? Since we are the "hands and feet of the Lord", we are the only Jesus many will ever see. Consider the following suggestions:

1. Forgiveness — When we forgive others it reminds all of us of His forgiving heart.

2. Kindness — Many people view God as cruel and unkind, especially if they've gone through difficult situations. When we are kind to others we demonstrate one of God's best attributes. Kindness is attractive and melts hearts like nothing else.

3. Generosity — Let's face it-God treats all of us better than we deserve. But many view the Church as self-absorbed, always asking for help but not giving it. People in the service industry label Christians stingy and demanding rather than "good tippers". We have many opportunities to make God look good to those who have alienated themselves from Him.

4. Love — You can go to church every time the doors are open but if you're not loving others God gets a black eye. His very essence is love, but many will never know it if we are not loving towards them. When others know we love them it s easier for them to accept the Father's love.

1 Corinthians. 10:31 "So whether you eat or drink, or whatever you do, do it all for the glory of God."

6
THE "TIPPING" POINT

As my wife and I sat in a booth at a favorite restaurant on a Sunday night, the noisy people at the next table finally left. The waitress knew us and stopped by to say she hated Sundays for that's when the Christians come in and demand a lot but tip little or not at all. We tried to assure her that we're not all like that, but her point of view was quite indicting since it was based on actual experience.

We sing songs and listen to messages about loving others and then leave church and often exhibit demanding, unfriendly attitudes towards those who serve us. This kind of behavior is not the witness God wants us to be. It would be more authentic to skip church and properly tip than attend service and short-change the server.

The "Tipping" point becomes a real disconnect for believers and non-believers. When we claim to be a follower of Christ but substitute tracts and notes saying "God loves you" instead of giving a healthy tip, we nullify our testimony and give the church a black eye.

I have four children who have all worked in the food industry. Their experience corroborates the waitress' report. This is a real issue that needs to be carefully considered.

Those who wait on us need all the kindness we can give. Our tips become their livelihood. As "Children of the King" we are expected to pass on our blessings.

Matthew 5: 14-16 (The Message) "Here's another way to put it: You're here to be light, bringing out the God-colors in the world. God is not a secret to be kept. We're going public with this, as public as a city on a hill. If I make you light-bearers, you don't think I'm going to hide you under a bucket, do you? I'm putting you on a light stand. Now that I've put you there on a hilltop, on a light stand—shine! Keep open house; be generous with your lives. By opening up to others, you'll prompt people to open up with God, this generous Father in heaven."

7
"THE POWER OF A NAME"

I was standing in line one day waiting to return an item I had purchased. It was obvious that the lady behind the customer service counter was not having a good day. In addition to dealing with dissatisfied customers, no doubt there were personnel tensions as she interacted with other employees. When it was my turn I said "Hi Mary." She immediately jerked and asked "how do you know my name?" I reminded her of the name tag she was wearing. It was like someone flipped a switch for she started to smile and the stress on her face and in her voice disappeared.

We like to be called by name and when others fail to do so, it can make us feel devalued. Church is a place where one expects to share their name or hear it spoken by another worshipper.

However, so often others greet us and never ask what our name is. They simply say "hello" or "glad you're here", but that's all. They don't mean to but it comes across as insincere and shallow when our name is omitted.

There are reasons why we do not use names. Sometimes we have already met the person but have forgotten their name.

Rather than embarrass ourselves further we choose to not ask. Also, as our communities become more global, we interact with people whose names are hard to pronounce or even hear. So, we tend to play it safe and keep our conversation on the surface.

If we are going to add value to others and demonstrate that we truly care, we must learn their names, no matter how long it takes. We all can do better at this---why not start today!

John 10: 27 (New Living Translation) My sheep listen to my voice; I know them, and they follow me

8
"GOOD NEWS OR BAD NEWS"

One day I had a tooth extracted. It did not come out easily, and I really felt it in spite of the extra Novocain. A week later it was still hurting, so I returned to the dentist and discovered I had a "dry socket". The Dr. treated it and instructed me to call in and let them know how I was doing, whether it was good or bad. When I called and said I was doing great, the nurse just didn't get it. She kept asking me if I was Ok or if I needed an appointment. I told her I was just letting them know everything was fine. She replied that I had "thrown her a curve" and she was not used to "my kind of call."

Now, I'm not faulting the nurse, but her reaction illustrates how attuned we are to bad news. In our instant-information world, one does not have to search for negative stories—they're everywhere. No matter what line of work you're in, you probably hear more complaints than you do compliments. We are conditioned to assume the worst scenario and can miss the good stuff all around us.

One more thought: When people see us coming toward them, do they think of us as good or bad news? We repel when we're sour and attract by being sweet. The world is dying for some good news, and we can choose to be it.

Proverbs 15:30 (New International Version) A cheerful look brings joy to the heart, and good news gives health to the bones.

9
"JEFF"

I was in the waiting room of my eye doctor one day and noticed that every few minutes a young technician, named Jeff, would look in and call out a name. Then he would introduce himself and treat the patient like they were a long, lost friend.

I had witnessed Jeff behaving this way several times. Patients who had their eyes bandaged or dilated were waiting to see the doctor. It's not very comfortable being in a room of strangers in that condition. But, when Jeff calls your name and takes you to a room for a test, he has a calming effect on you and restores your dignity.

Finally, he called my name. Back in his room I told him how he impacts the atmosphere of the clinic by his kind mannerisms. He accepted the compliment and continued to focus not on himself but on me. It was no surprise to find a Bible sitting on his desk and to hear him describe his job as a ministry.

We have a choice—to be a thermometer or a thermostat. We can simply adapt to our environment or we can change it. Kind words accompanied by a smile comprise the highest form of Christian witness. People will never listen to you if they don't like you. They must hear the music before they'll listen to your words.

Ephesians 4: 32 (New International Version) Be kind and compassionate to one another, forgiving each other, just as in Christ God forgave you.

10
"GET BUSY LIVIN' OR GET BUSY DYIN'

In the movie "The Shawshank Redemption," Red, played by Morgan Freeman, there's a moment of timeless insight when he says, "We either get busy livin' or get busy dyin'."

It's a new year, and we are busy negotiating through the demands of life. Challenges of the old year follow us into this one, and so we make choices as to how to spend our time. Will we focus on dead issues or direct our energies toward living up to our potential?

We can turn inward and see how bad things are for us, or we can look outward and make things better for others. No matter what we are experiencing, there are people all around us who would trade places with us in a heartbeat. But, we'll never see them if we only look in the mirror.

Since we're going to be busy anyway, why not make every day count by treating others better than they deserve. Most people you meet are trying to cope with money, health and relationship issues. We can make a positive difference when we focus on livin' for that points us to a Savior who makes it all worthwhile, both now and later.

Philippians 1: 21 (New King James Version) For to me, to live is Christ, and to die is gain.

11
"TIME FOR YOU TO PAY"

I was having a quick lunch in a Chinese restaurant one day. At a nearby table sat a woman with two young children and an infant. Overhearing some of their conversation I deduced that it was a blended family of sorts. Finally, the daughter, probably about 8 years old, looked straight at her mom and unabashedly said "Time for you to pay."

When God the Father sent His only son to this world, it was the most expensive Christmas gift ever given. The expense of our salvation began long before Calvary's Cross in a manger out back of an overcrowded inn. The world had been in spiritual darkness long enough—it was time for someone to pay. Imagine what it was like to give your only son away to people who could accept or reject Him. The same person that brought joy to our world was also greatly missed in heaven. But someone had to pay if true light was to penetrate humanity. Jesus stepped up and made the first installment on our salvation.

Remember, all gifts cost. Someone pays before we enjoy; whether it be presents or food or gift certificates, there is a price that must be satisfied before we can accept the gift. Don't forget to thank Him for the greatest gift you'll ever receive.

Galatians 4: 4 (New International Version) But when the right time came, God sent his Son, born of a woman, subject to the law.

12
"THE POWER OF ACCEPTANCE"

We have no idea how we impact other people when we accept them. Most of us walk around with some measure of inferiority. So, when we're accepted it helps us to overcome our feelings of "not measuring up" so we can live a normal life. The fear of rejection causes us to perform far below our capability resulting in being misjudged.

The first Christmas is a clear model of acceptance. When teenage Mary was informed that she was to be the mother of the Messiah, she could have said "No way—I'm not going to give up my life for an unexpected pregnancy. Besides, who's going to believe this ridiculous story of a virgin birth?"

Joseph makes himself vulnerable when he accepts the position of stand-in dad. He knows he's not the biological father and yet refuses to abandon Mary. The power demonstrated by these young parents lies in the fact they accepted their situation knowing that God would, somehow, make a way for them.

Whatever you're facing right now, accept it, not with resignation but with resolve that God knows where you are and will bring good out of it. When others observe us in difficult and awkward situations, our ability to accept has a touch of the divine and that's powerful.

Luke 1: 34-38 (The Message) Mary said to the angel, "But how? I've never slept with a man." The angel answered, "The Holy Spirit will come upon you, the power of the Highest hover over you; Therefore, the child you bring to birth will be called Holy, Son of God. And did you know that your cousin Elizabeth conceived a son, old as she is? Everyone called her barren, and here she is six months pregnant! Nothing, you see, is impossible with God." And Mary said, "Yes, I see it all now: I'm the Lord's maid, ready to serve. Let it be with me just as you say."

13
"THE BIGGEST NO BRAINER IN THE HISTORY OF EARTH"

Occasionally I hear an interesting ad on XM Radio from a guy who is in the mortgage finance business. His pitch always includes the words, "this is the biggest no-brainer in the history of earth." This phrase sounds quite braggadocios at first, but after hearing it several times, we realize the speaker actually believes it and that sells.

It's Christmastime and many are trying to sell us stuff with incredible claims of how good their product is. Their goal is to make us want it so much that we buy it without much deliberation. Even in these tough economic times many will make purchases that, if they had taken time to think about it, would have passed on the deal.

For those of us who have been raised in the Christian faith, believing in and celebrating the birth of Christ is "the biggest no-brainer in the history of earth." We simply buy into the biblical story—it rings true and we accept it.

Many people, in our pluralistic world, experience difficulty believing in the simple Christmas story. Some living in North America, believe it or not, have never been exposed to the story of Jesus coming to earth. Others have heard it many times but have been swept up in the secularization of the holiday. They're just too busy to even think about it.

One thing for sure—Dec. 25 will be here before we know it. Christ wants those who are called by His name to not forget His birthday. It's the "biggest no-brainer in the history of earth."

14
"DIMINISHING SUNLIGHT"

In my part of the world, it is definitely fall as the leaves on the trees turn glorious golds, grape-plum reds and burnt oranges. Almost everywhere you look the landscape is full of color that supersedes the rendition of any artist.

Just a few more days and the leaves will be gone to be recycled on the ground or raked and bagged by some family member. It would seem that cooling temperatures would cause this annual change. But, science informs us that it is diminishing sunlight which sends a signal to turn and, ultimately, detach from the tree.

From time to time, all of us experience diminishing sunlight. It may come as the result of failing health or possible injury. Loss of job and income can certainly darken our outlook. Broken and strained relationships rob us of joy and make our lives grey. Living with increasing shadows requires us to relish light moments. It makes us more aware that people surrounding us live in the dark more than they would like and seem to have little hope.

When we go through tough times, understand that God is bringing out colors of character that would otherwise never be seen. People are observing our demeanor more than we know, especially when we keep moving in spite of setbacks. God is painting a picture to a fallen world that cannot be accomplished when everything goes right.

Hold on tightly to His hand—you will bud again.

Consider this old gospel song:

Standing somewhere in the shadows you'll find Jesus
He's the only one who cares and understands
Standing somewhere in the shadows you will find Him
And you'll know Him by the nail prints in His hand.

15
"NON-ZONED AREA"

Most of us, at one time or another, have experienced something like the following: You go into a restaurant—they are very busy, but that's good because it usually indicates great food and good service. You try to assist the greeter (who is also checking people out) by seating yourself after she points to a table being cleaned. You sit down and watch as new people come and have their orders taken before you are even offered a menu. You try to be patient for it's obvious that the servers are doing their best. Yet, as you continue to sit, unattended, it becomes more difficult to stay cool. It is unfair—after all, you have appointments, too. It's not anyone's fault necessarily. You just seem to be sitting in a non-zoned area— like no one is assigned to your booth.

When we go through times of trial and disappointment, it is easy to think God has forgotten us. Others "seem" to be doing OK, even flourishing. Their lives go on as planned while ours seem to be on hold, even stopped. What do we do when we see ourselves in a non-zoned area?

Understand—God has not lost track of you. His GPS (Global Positioning System) has been active and accurate since the beginning of time. He not only knows where you are but how you feel about where you are.

Realize that others surrounding you are not the cause for your situation. Everyone is trying to navigate through this world the best they can, so do not blame anyone for your predicament.

When help comes (and it will) be grateful and kind to the messenger. God uses many people to help us through life. Step back and you'll see His hand.

Each day you will encounter family, friends and even strangers who feel abandoned and helpless. Don't pass them by without attempting to lighten their day. The best way to show God's love is to share our love first.

Matthew. 25: 40 (The Message) Then those 'sheep' are going to say, 'Master, what are you talking about? When did we ever see you hungry and feed you, thirsty and give you a drink? And when did we ever see you sick or in prison and come to you?' Then the King will say, 'I'm telling the solemn truth: Whenever you did one of these things to someone overlooked or ignored, that was me—you did it to me.

16
"ANOTHER SENTENCE WOULD HAVE MADE IT OK"

Understanding others is a life-long project. Even when we think we know another person we can be fooled and deeply hurt by what they say or don't say to us. Of course, we cannot speak for others; however, we can pay closer attention to what we ourselves say and how we say it.

Communication is one of the great challenges of life. Experts say that 80% of marriage conflicts are a result of faulty communication. Anytime we are talking to others, whether it is in person or on the phone or an Email message, it's easy to be misunderstood. So often just one more sentence or phrase would soften the tone and cause the hearer to feel loved and respected.

For example, suppose you're talking to someone and you say, "You'll have to get someone else to help you, I'm busy." It may be true that you are busy and just stating the fact. But, the receiver of your message feels disrespected and marginalized. A better way would be to add another sentence like, "I'm sorry I can't help you right now— I sure hope I can help in the future."

Understand; you may be a kind, sensitive person. But, when a problem comes along and you don't want to deal with it but because of your position are required to, you may step away from your usual calm manner and just bulldoze through in order to say what has to be said. Don't forget to add one more sentence to let the other person know you really care. It is critical to remember this to maintain good relationships and to act like Jesus.

Colossians 4: 6 (The Message) Be gracious in your speech. The goal is to bring out the best in others in a conversation, not put them down, not cut them out.

17
"CHANGE YOUR FILTER"

It's that time of the year again when you need to turn on the heat source in your house. If you have a forced-air furnace you probably should change your filter so that it will allow unrestricted distribution of warmth throughout your home. The slightest blockage can greatly reduce the effectiveness of the air-flow.

The filter on our minds also needs periodic changing. We live in a negative world that tends to gum up our thinking. Life's challenges can hinder our ability to be positive and open to new ideas. We can find ourselves living with the news cycle rather than focusing on more important matters, such as relationships and personal spiritual health.

Just as central heating and cooling sends conditioned air to all parts of the house, likewise, our filtered minds send messages to others that can impact the atmosphere for good or for bad. A negative word or look can discourage people more than we know. On the other hand, an affirmation and smile can make everyone feel better about life.

The choice is yours to make. Go ahead and refresh your thinking—everyone will be glad you did.

Philippians 4: 8 (The Message) Summing it all up, friends, I'd say you'll do best by filling your minds and meditating on things true, noble, reputable, authentic, compelling, gracious—the best, not the worst; the beautiful, not the ugly; things to praise, not things to curse.

18
"HERO UNIT"

Traveling by car brings extra wear and tear resulting in a higher probability of car trouble. It happened to me one day as I headed to the office. I was on a busy freeway, and it was pouring rain. Out of nowhere my car began to vibrate, and I pulled over to discover a flat tire.

Not having a change of clothes I tried to avoid changing the tire myself. I called my road service company and found out my coverage had expired. I then called my insurance agent to see if I was covered, but the agent's office was not open. Just then my phone rang and a friend told me to try a "Hero Unit." He explained that these units travel the freeways of the greater Atlanta area helping stranded motorists. So, I called 9-1-1 and was told I was too far south of the city to get help. I subsequently discovered that it would cost me $75 to have a towing service come out and change my tire.

I had just decided to change the tire myself when a large yellow truck with flashing lights pulled up behind me. It was the Hero Unit. The kind man explained that due to the construction he had to travel further south than usual. He changed my tire at no charge, and I was on my way in just a few minutes. I see how they got their name.

To someone, you are a hero. You may not look or feel like one but you are one just the same. There are people experiencing physical, marital, mental and emotional breakdowns all around you. They need someone to listen and empathize. We may not know what to say but we can be there to support and share in their time of need. Slow down and let God use you today.

Matthew 5:16 (Contemporary English Version) Make your light shine, so that
others will see the good that you do and will praise your Father in heaven.

19
"LOVE YOU"

Most of us have times when we feel unloved and underappreciated. It's part of living in a "fallen world" and in uncertain times. We may mentally know that we're accepted and loved, but our feelings change with the circumstances.

When someone tells us they love us it is a gift to be cherished. Many find it difficult to express themselves—so, when they make the effort to connect we need to openly receive it. By doing so we are more likely to pass it on to another person waiting for affirmation.

Some people can go a long time on one expression of praise—many cannot. Since we dwell in a climate of negativity and indifference, it is important that we remind our friends and family that we, in fact, really love them. Kindness, generosity and patience are all keys in spreading love. However, to state it means we make ourselves vulnerable, not knowing if anyone will reciprocate.

Let us never forget that our very existence is predicated on God's love for us. He demonstrates it every day by allowing us to negotiate our way through life with His constant help and care. So often He uses others to supply our deep, emotional needs.

The entire story of redemption, from leaving heaven, being ridiculed and belittled, the merciless beatings, the crucifixion and abandonment by the Father—all of this is saying "Love You."

John 3: 16-17 (The Message) This is how much God loved the world: He gave his Son, his one and only Son. And this is why: so that no one need be destroyed; by believing in him, anyone can have a whole and lasting life. God didn't go to all the trouble of sending his Son merely to point an accusing finger, telling the world how bad it was. He came to help, to put the world right again.

20
"TAKE AND LEAVE"

People everywhere are carrying burdens. We may not see them, but nevertheless they are very real.

An old gospel song says "Take your burdens to the Lord and leave them there." Most of us have no problem taking our burdens to God, but leaving them is another matter. We seem to think that we can handle them, as though we are super human. This false pride robs us of available peace.

How do we leave our burdens? Well, we must keep on dumping our cares and concerns on the One who told us to cast all of our cares upon Him. It's not a one-time act but a sacred habit.

Secondly, leaving our problems does not mean we go off and sit on a hillside and wait for our Master to take us to heaven. We stay engaged in our responsibilities and duties while continuing to pass on our worries to a Savior who loves us more than we know.

Lastly, sometimes we must carry our burdens for a while. We provide the man or woman—God provides the grace. The Lord knows how far we can go and will bring remedy in His time.

1 Peter 5: 7 (New Living Translation) Give all your worries and cares to God, for he cares about you.

21
"THE DISCIPLINE OF DELAY"

No one I know likes to wait. We live in an "instant society", which makes all of us antsier than we used to be. Yet, we spend a lot of time waiting in traffic, in the grocery store and on each other.

Some of our waiting is intentional when we delay a purchase or activity. We simply discipline ourselves to save enough money, so we can pay cash or delay our vacation until the off season rates begin. The benefits of this kind of delay more than outweigh the discomfort of waiting.

Much of the delay we encounter, though, is out of our hands. We wait on answers from prospective employers or the results from lab work. We wait on God to show us what to do or where to go. The longer we wait the greater the discipline that's imposed upon us. We wish we could speed things up, get a definite answer and move on with our lives. Most often we must simply press on believing God has reasons for postponing closure. We will understand it later in this life or the next.

So, as one who is quite familiar with waiting on God, I encourage you to keep on trusting and believing that He will see you through--we are being shaped into His likeness.

As a great friend of mine says, "better days ahead."

Jeremiah 29: 11 (New Living Translation) For I know the plans I have for you," says the Lord. "They are plans for good and not for disaster, to give you a future and a hope.

22
"360 PROTECTION"

The fact that you're reading this is indicative of God's grace and mercy. How many times did the Lord protect you this past week as you went through the intersection on red? Ate food prepared in an unclean restaurant? Accidentally used the wrong medicine?

God's angels work overtime for some of us. Guarding our homes as we sleep and steering damaging storms another direction are samples of providential care.

As for people who are in wrecks, suffer food poisoning, are burglarized or hit by a storm, I do not have any answers except to say that He will be with us no matter what happens. The point is we need to be mindful of His surrounding protection and to express gratitude for all the unseen work our Savior does for us.

Since He has us covered, let us not fear the future. Keep focused on Him—He will surely bring you out.

Psalms 3: 3-5 (The Message) But you, God, shield me on all sides; You ground my feet, you lift my head high; With all my might I shout up to God, His answers thunder from the holy

mountain. I stretch myself out. I sleep. Then I'm up again—
rested, tall and steady...

23
"WHAT DO YOU DO IN THE MEANTIME?"

Life is made up of times of waiting for something to happen, for an important call or, perhaps, the results from the lab work ordered by our doctor. The time we spend when no answer is found or no solution is forthcoming can be called the "meantime".

What do you do in the meantime? Many worry and fret, but experience has shown these responses to be nonproductive. Another tactic is to try even harder to resolve the problem on our own, which usually leads to more frustration. Truth is: we don't know how long we'll have to wait before our circumstances change and God answers our prayers.

So, what do we do? I'm no expert, but allow me to share what I'm learning. First, be honest with yourself and those close to you. The "meantime" can be quite mean as we struggle to make sense of it all. Being honest does not mean crying on everyone's shoulder or pretending to be super spiritual. Rather, be yourself and accept the genuine support from friends and family.

Secondly, you must ingest more positive stuff than usual. God's word, uplifting stories, positive people and inspiring music can do wonders for your outlook.

Lastly, do not give up on God. Walking in the dark is scary and treading water is tiring, but keep moving. Better days are ahead. God knows where you are because He's right beside you. Amen!

Psalm 37: 5-7a (The Message) Open up before God, keep nothing back; he'll do whatever needs to be done: He'll validate your life in the clear light of day and stamp you with approval at high noon.

Quiet down before God, be prayerful before him.

24
"WHAT JUST HAPPENED?"

I had just come off the freeway and was trying to turn against the oncoming traffic. I started out into the lane and then suddenly stopped as a pickup truck was speeding toward me. Since the car behind me was also trying to advance, I had no room to back up which left me a little bit extended into the path of traffic. The driver in the pickup had ample room to negotiate around me but became very mad and made several hand gestures which indicated his displeasure that I had impeded his progress. He was completely ignorant of what caused me to be in his lane and must have assumed I "messed him up" on purpose.

As we live our lives, we are often in the dark of "what just happened". We encounter people acting differently, and we tend to judge them too harshly or question their actions without knowing what has transpired in their immediate past. Of course, there is no way of knowing all the events and situations others are experiencing, and so we must ask God to help us to not jump to conclusions and to assume the best rather than the worst.

This is no small task and requires moment by moment monitoring. We cannot change what others do or even know why they do it. But, we can definitely improve the atmosphere around us when we recognize our ignorance and pray for God's wisdom.

Ephesians 4:32 NLT Instead, be kind to each other, tenderhearted, forgiving one another, just as God through Christ has forgiven you.

25
"PREACHING WITHOUT A PULPIT"

Being a "preacher" for the last 39 plus years has molded me into one who respects and esteems those who proclaim the "good news" from the pulpit (lectern, sacred desk). For sure, preaching is a unique form of communication, different from any other kind of presentation. But the fact is: relatively little time is actually spent in a worship setting. Mostly, our days are spent engaged in other activities than listening to someone expound the scripture.

Experts say that 85% of communication does not involve words but is made up of tone and body language. That means we really do spend a lot of time preaching without a pulpit. People watch our faces and observe our moods. When they do not match our words a disconnect occurs. We inadvertently strengthen non believers' assertion of too many hypocrites in the church.

So, how do we preach without a pulpit? First, smile as much as you can. People will never be attracted to the Savior until they first are attracted to you.

Secondly, lower your voice a little and speak gently. It's not only disarming but also provides poise and a greater sense of dignity.

Thirdly, speak non-judgmentally to others. No one likes to be labeled or talked down to, especially if they sense you may consider yourself godlier than them.

Lastly, be real and natural. The world has had its fill of stereotypical Christianity. Authenticity is what people are looking for—it's the invitation of our message.

Matthew 5: 14-16 (The Message) … You're here to be light, bringing out the God-colors in the world. God is not a secret to be kept. We're going public with this, as public as a city on a hill. If I make you light-bearers, you don't think I'm going to hide you under a bucket, do you? I'm putting you on a light stand. Now that I've put you there on a hilltop, on a light stand—shine! Keep open house; be generous with your lives. By opening up to others, you'll prompt people to open up with God, this generous Father in heaven.

26
"PEACE ON A POWERLINE"

I sat on my porch one day and watched as three little birds were perched peacefully on a power line during a summer storm. No matter how much the wind blew or lightening flashed or thunder rumbled this trio seemed unimpressed by it all. They were quite at home in this threatening environment, as stable as if they were 25 feet lower on the ground.

One does not have to live long to experience storms in their life. They are inevitable as long as we walk the face of this earth. How are we to remain calm and quiet while life's challenges keep on coming?

Just like the birds, we must know that our Creator is in control and will protect us from harm. He not only knows the number of hairs on our head but sees every hop we make.

Secondly, storms will not last forever, no matter how long they seem to go on and on. Our Heavenly Father knows how much we can handle, so hold on to Him and His people.

Lastly, keep a low profile (stay humble) and allow the storms to blow over you. Just like trees that bend in the wind, stay flexible and be ready to make any changes God may want for your life. The sun is about to shine again.

IS. 26: 3 (New King James Version) "You will keep him in perfect peace, Whose mind is stayed on You, Because he trusts in You."

27
"HE CERTAINLY CHEWS WELL"

Remember when you were learning to drive? No doubt someone told you to keep your eyes on the road and not on other vehicles, buildings or pedestrians. Your instructor knew that whatever you focus on you'll head toward.

We do live in a negative world where bad news comes at us right and left through the media. In order to stay positive we have to ingest good stuff each day by what we read, watch and listen to. The people we hang out with will greatly influence our outlook on life. If they are negative "handwringers", we will become worriers too. But, when our friends have a positive attitude toward life it is fun to be around them—make sure others want to be close to you because you are a winner and not a whiner.

It takes no effort at all to see the deficit in other people or ideas. However, seeing the good in others is doable if you are looking for it.

When our 1st son was about two years old, he lived with us in Nairobi, Kenya. Our Field Director, Jerry, and his wife Bunny, had dinner with us one evening. We wanted our son to be on his best behavior but he chose to not cooperate at the dinner table. He cried, threw his food on the floor and embarrassed his parents. But Jerry always saw the good in others and said, in the midst of our son's tirade, "He certainly chews well."

Find the good today---it's all around you if you'll look for it.

Philippians 4: 8 (The Message) Summing it all up, friends, I'd say you'll do best by filling your minds and meditating on things true, noble, reputable, authentic, compelling, gracious—the best, not the worst; the beautiful, not the ugly; things to praise, not things to curse.

28
"WHY DID THE TURTLE CROSS THE ROAD?"

I was driving on the freeway one day when I came upon a box turtle crossing the road. He was in the middle of the outside lane. I missed him and so did the car behind me, but I'm not sure if he made it all the way.

I'm quite familiar with turtles having had them as pets when I was a young boy. Turtles are slow and usually stay in safe areas. To see one out on the road was a shock for he was definitely out of his comfort zone. This crawling reptile was resolute and determined to move across the lanes of oncoming traffic. He was moving as fast as a turtle can in 93 degree heat.

Why did the turtle cross the road? The answer is simple yet profound—to get to where he wanted to be.

Getting to where we want to be is often risky and sometimes dangerous. But, we will never achieve much in life if we hide in our shell and just let the world pass by. Sometimes we just have to take a chance, go against the traffic and not stop until we make our destination.

Following the Lord is also challenging. Many times we find

ourselves going against the flow of things, crossing barriers that seem impossible. The good news is that God knows where He is leading us—we'll make it if we keep moving.

Jeremiah 29: 11 (New International Version) For I know the plans I have for you," declares the LORD, "plans to prosper you and not to harm you, plans to give you hope and a future.

29
"LIVING ON BORROWED TIME"

The amount of consumer debt in the USA is nearly $2.4 trillion in 2010--that's $7,800 debt per person. This is a number beyond our comprehension. People borrow to buy homes, cars and an education. Far too much stuff is purchased with plastic which costs a whole lot more via the minimum payment plan.

I've heard the phrase "living on borrowed time" all of my life, particularly when it refers to someone who has passed a certain age or is dealing with a disease. But, in reality, all of us are living on borrowed time. We became terminal the moment we were born.

To borrow suggests we don't own it ourselves—it belongs to someone else. While we have it we're responsible to protect it and keep it in good condition. Borrowed things will one day have to be returned to the owner.

We value individual freedom and self-determinism. However, followers of Christ recognize that they operate under divine authority.

Therefore, it's vital that they maximize their short time on earth by doing things that will last forever-- like sharing the gospel with friends and family.

These words were posted in my grandparents' house:

Only one life, twill soon be past
Only what's done for Christ, will last.

James 4:14 (New Living Translation) - How do you know what your life will be like tomorrow? Your life is like the morning fog—it's here a little while, then it's gone.

30
"THE LORD WILLING"

I recall my grandmother saying things like, "We plan to go shopping tomorrow ....the Lord willing," or, "We'll be going to our oldest son's house for Thanksgiving ...the Lord willing." Life was much slower for us then, living in the country on a small farm in the 1950's. One did not shop or travel without some planning and forethought since there were always the chores to do and no 24/7 stores.

Our lifestyles have drastically changed in the last five decades or so. Since we can travel more we tend to do things more impulsively, even with the high price of gas. It's easy to become overextended with "too many irons in the fire". The quality of life can go down quickly when we get too busy.

"...The Lord willing" is a good reminder that we who follow Him do so at His pleasure. In other words, we keep Him in the picture as we order and prioritize our lives. Of course we want His blessing on our activities—we need His help moment by moment.

Verbalizing "...the Lord willing" helped to keep my grandparents close to God. It was a humble reminder that He is in charge, not us. For Believers, this concept is timeless.

Hebrews 6: 3 (New Living Translation) And so, God willing, we will move forward to further understanding.

31
"INDIVIDUAL RESULTS MAY VARY"

I find disclaimers in advertising to be quite humorous at times. It seems like more time is spent telling us what may go wrong than what could go right. Sometimes the testimonials are so unbelievable that we are told "individual results may vary". That kind of lets the advertiser off the hook in case it does not work.

In spiritual matters, individual results do vary. We're all unique; at different places in our lives. Some approach God and church with real enthusiasm—others are somewhat skeptical, hoping their past negative experiences can be proven wrong. So, they may be slow to get involved, to fully embrace "organized religion".

The good news is Christ wants a relationship with us personally. He knows us better than we know ourselves, and is very patient as we serve Him the best we know how.

While Bible reading, prayer, worship and service are all vital to our maturing, we will tend to engage these activities in our own way. Our life is not the same as our friends. "Cookie-Cutter Christianity" has never been valid.

The main thing is that we seek Him with our whole heart,

whether we've walked with God for 50 years or are just now thinking about being a Believer. The final result is peace in this life and a place in heaven.

Philippians 2: 13 (The Message) Be energetic in your life of salvation, reverent and sensitive before God. That energy is God's energy, an energy deep within you, God himself willing and working at what will give him the most pleasure.

32
"TESTED ON CHECKOUT LINE 3"

Invariably, when I encourage others to act a certain way, I am tested on the very same thing, usually before the day has ended.

While at work, I wrote that we should try to make it a great day for all who see and talk to us. Before I returned home from the office my wife asked me to stop by the store and pick up a "few things". Most husbands know that a few things can sometimes require more than one cart.

Anyway, I'm standing in Checkout Line 3, waiting for the customer ahead to check out. Apparently, she had a split order but failed to place a dividing stick in the middle. So, the nice young cashier scanned more than was desired in the first order. Then came the painful process of "putting back" stuff that should be charged in order number two. The nervous employee kept apologizing to the lady; she instructed him to direct his remarks to me. Fortunately, I recognized my test and determined to stay calm and keep smiling.

The ordeal finally ended and I headed to the parking lot. The lady who had been in front of me was now parked beside me. She came by and said, "Let me return your cart. After all, it's the least I can do."

Living out what we believe and teach is not always easy. However, it's the only thing others will see that trumps their cynicism and doubt.

Matt. 5: 14-16 (The Message) Here's another way to put it: You're here to be light, bringing out the God-colors in the world. God is not a secret to be kept. We're going public with this, as public as a city on a hill. If I make you light-bearers, you don't think I'm going to hide you under a bucket, do you? I'm putting you on a light stand. Now that I've put you there on a hilltop, on a light stand—shine! Keep open house; be generous with your lives. By opening up to others, you'll prompt people to open up with God, this generous Father in heaven.

33
"LEFT BEHIND"

Have you ever felt left behind? Maybe it was an amusement park where you were not tall enough to get on a ride, or you were not good enough for the neighborhood baseball team. Perhaps you were told by the choir director that you were just a kid and could not sing in the choir even though you knew you were better than anyone seated in the loft.

Ever-changing technology tends to cause many of us to feel bypassed. We try to keep up, but the changes are coming too fast. We look around and it "seems like" everyone else is moving ahead and we are not. It's easy to feel sorry for ourselves which hinders any forward progress.

Many hold the view that anyone left behind must be inferior or second class. However, history indicates that, in many situations, those left behind were the most reliable people; they could be trusted to do their duty no matter what. For example, a military commander would leave some of his best people to guard the fort while he led others on various missions. When Jesus was dying on the cross, He entrusted John to take care of His mother Mary. The gospel according to John contains all we need to know to reach heaven.

We are not on this earth by accident. The fact that we're

alive right now means God has a profound purpose for our existence. He is counting on us to "hang in" as long as it takes. He is using you to impact others for God and for good more than you think.

One more thought: when He comes, you will not be left behind.

Matt. 25: 23 (New International Version) His master replied, "Well done, good and faithful servant! You have been faithful with a few things; I will put you in charge of many things. Come and share your master's happiness!"

34
"SALUTING THE SACRED"

I had the privilege, one day, to witness an event most civilians do not ever see. As I was leaving a major military installation, I noticed people standing at attention, looking across a large field. Those in uniform saluted and others dressed in "civies" placed their right hand over their heart. Soldiers driving by stopped, got out of their cars and saluted as the US flag was being taken down for the night. It was a moving scene as respect and honor were given to a symbol of liberty and freedom, one that has cost the lives of thousands of heroes.

We live in a day where "sacred things" like the Bible and the cross are often disrespected and belittled. We forget that these two representations of the Christian faith have not only stood the test of time but have also been defended by unassuming, faithful people across the globe who have given their lives in the service of their Captain.

It is time for those who consider Christ their personal Savior to elevate their sense of the Holy and to counter frivolous attitudes towards sacred things. The world is crying out for this kind of Christianity.

The songwriter says it best:

"So I'll cherish, the old rugged cross.
Till my trophies at last I lay down.
I will cling to the old rugged cross,
And exchange it someday for a crown."

35
"WRONG ASSUMPTIONS"

I was given directions for a scheduled appointment. The person talking on the phone to me was quite confident he was guiding me where I needed to be. The problem was, I found out later, he assumed I was heading west when, in fact, I was going east. Therefore, his instructions were totally invalid.

We make a lot of assumptions about people. For example, we can surmise that someone is unfriendly, not knowing they are experiencing some kind of physical or emotional or even mental pain. It is true, people everywhere are carrying burdens. They might not be obvious but they are there, none the less.

The Bible makes it quite clear that we should avoid judging others. We usually do not have enough information to really understand what another person is dealing with. In addition, we often do not know "where they are coming from" so we completely misjudge them.

It's a fine balance of helping and hindering others. You can never go wrong by praying more for those around you.

Matthew 7: 1 (The Message) "Don't pick on people, jump on their failures, criticize their faults— unless, of course, you want the same treatment. That critical spirit has a way of boomeranging."

36
"THE VALUE OF GOLDEN RULE LIVING"

It seems like every day the price of gold increases. As world economies fluctuate in relation to each other, gold just keeps on rising in value. For now, it is something you can count on.

A much more precious commodity is how we treat each other. Most of the time we are self-absorbed, trying to excel even in uncertain times. Climbing the corporate ladder, so to speak, can make us rather indifferent to others who may be stuck on a rung, wanting to go to the next step but unable. We can think "Why can't they just move forward like I did?"

We know how we want to be treated but can easily forget that others desire the same respect and patience. We get caught up in our policies and procedures which often are cold and inhospitable to the very people we're supposed to be helping.

As you and I mature in years, hopefully we begin to realize that the way we treat others is ultimately the way we treat our Lord. Healthy relationships are necessary for a happy life. Adding value to others is an investment that will pay eternal dividends.

Luke 6: 31 (The Message) "Here is a simple rule of thumb for behavior: Ask yourself what you want people to do for you; then grab the initiative and do it for them!"

37
"TOO CLOSE TO CALL"

National and state elections are often very competitive. With 24 hour TV coverage we're probably getting more information than we need or want regarding the contest. Repeatedly we hear the words "too close to call" to describe the short and long term results. Polls are all over the map regarding who will win or not.

Situations in life are also often "too close to call". In other words, we don't know what will happen, how the challenges in our life will be resolved. For those of us who live by faith, believing God has our best interests at heart, we learn to be content without knowing the outcome. It's a daily/hourly, sometimes moment by moment choice to trust that God knows what He's doing even though we don't.

A quick review of the more prominent Bible stories reveals many "too close to call" scenarios. In fact, often the odds were totally against the hero of the story, yet God intervened and won the day.

Hold on to Him for His answer—it's likely already on the way!

Ps. 37: 7a NLT Be still in the presence of the LORD, and wait patiently for him to act.

38
"KEEPING POWER"

When I was growing up I heard my grandparents repeatedly thank God for His "keeping power". It sounded OK to me, and I accepted it as one of the Lord's regular duties.

Now, after walking with the Lord for many years and experiencing all sorts of life's challenges, I'm beginning to fully understand just how powerful God is, that He can keep us from falling no matter how rough the terrain may be.

One of the definitions of power is to control and influence. "Keeping" is described as the act of looking after or caring for somebody. This is what our Creator does for us. He influences us to make the right decisions, to hold steady even when we want to run away and hide.

We tend to think of "power" as in conquering or overwhelming strength. God's keeping power may be His greatest attribute for He reinforces our faith to hold on until He's ready to answer our prayers. Our part is to think about Him which leads to more peace. Sure beats thinking about yourself.

You will keep him in perfect peace, Whose mind is stayed on You, Because he trusts in You. IS. 26: 3 New King James Version

39
"I WISH I COULD GIVE MORE"

We understand that Christmas is a time of giving. Most of us are beneficiaries of the giving spirit of our friends and family. It's fun to buy and make gifts for others. Commercialism tries to obscure the real meaning of the season; however, it does prompt us to give our loved ones gifts that, in a perfect world, we might give them all year long.

No matter how much money or time we have we often wish we could give more. Financial realities tend to limit our ability to give, although millions of people will charge through the month and pay next year. For them, Christmas lasts longer than they would like.

"I wish I could give more" is a phrase never thought of or spoken by God the Father. For when He gave His only son as our Christmas present, it was the best gift ever given. All the money in the world could never afford such a present. He is the Gift that keeps on giving even when we forget Him.

Like any true gift, Jesus was given with no thought of receiving a present in return. All we have to do is to make room for Him in our heart. That's the gift He wants the most.

This is how much God loved the world: He gave his Son, his one and only Son. And this is why: so that no one need be destroyed; by believing in him, anyone can have a whole and lasting life. Jn. 3: 16 (MSG)

40
"STILL A CHRISTIAN"

The story is told about a man who served for 35 years in Africa as a bishop for his church. The day came for his retirement, so he returned to his beloved England. Because of his office he was invited to a party with other dignitaries of the country. Having lived on another continent for so many years, he had lost contact with many people and was trying to fit in again. A lady, who obviously knew the bishop, began talking to him. Nothing she said gave him the faintest clue as to who she was. Finally the bishop asked "what is your sister doing these days?" The reply was, "Oh, she's still queen."

If you've lived for 20 or more years, you know that our world is changing faster than ever. We come and go, change careers and try to adjust to all the new ways of doing things. Our faith and belief system is constantly challenged by our ever-increasing secularized society. To be able to say that we're still serving our Lord, believing Him for daily blessing and trusting Him, even in the dark, is no small feat. It is His grace that makes it all possible.

In this month of gift giving, we have the opportunity to give our family and friends an unwrapped, open to see life of solid devotion to Jesus. He is the reason for all our seasons.

Ps. 37: 28 (NLT) For the Lord loves justice, and he will never abandon the godly. He will keep them safe forever...

41
"SUSPENDED"

The word "suspend" has several different meanings. One that affects all of us is "to stop something or make something ineffective, usually for a short time". Having your driver's license suspended or membership privileges to an organization curtailed are not pleasant experiences.

Most people encounter this reality in more benign ways. Still, it represents change that is not always easy to do, like suspending certain eating habits in favor of better health or quitting a debilitating habit which may have controlled you for many years. Life is full of delays that we'll probably never understand, so we find ourselves in a state of suspension.

One definition we must never forget is "to hang something from above". That's what our Lord did when He was suspended on the cross between heaven and earth for your sins and mine. May we never lose sight that "this world is not our home, we're just passing through". Amen!

1 Corinthians 13:12 (MSG) We don't yet see things clearly. We're squinting in a fog, peering through a mist. But it won't be long before the weather clears and the sun shines bright!

We'll see it all then, see it all as clearly as God sees us, knowing him directly just as he knows us!

42
"THE UNSEEN HAND"

Years ago I attended a gospel music event which included an amateur contest. Group after group took the stage to sing their best song for their fans and friends. Some of the quartets and ensembles were quite good—others not so much. They came out in their performing outfits and arrived by custom made motor coaches, spending a lot of their own money just to sing one song.

Finally, a little boy about 11 years old, dressed in a dark suit, came to the center of the platform and wowed the audience with his rendition of an old gospel song, "The Unseen Hand". As soon as I heard him sing the first verse, I knew he would win. He did!

Words to the song go like this:

There is an unseen hand to me
That leads through ways I can not see.
While going through this world of woe
This hand still leads me as I go.

CHORUS:
I'm trusting to the unseen hand
That guides me through this weary land;
And some sweet day I'll reach that strand,
Still guided by the unseen hand.

We walk by faith and not by sight. Keep holding on as if your life is on the line---it is!

Ephesians 3:12 (MSG) "When we trust in him, we're free to say whatever needs to be said, bold to go wherever we need to go."

43
"WORKING YOUR WAY THROUGH"

Work is a four letter word we cannot avoid, although we keep trying. Certainly, all work and no play or anything else is not fun. We need balance in our lives which requires continual vigilance.

Life gives us constant challenges that we must solve. Often, we try to ignore them or find ourselves on a detour around problems. Still, the best way is not avoidance but to simply work through them. This usually involves getting help from others, including "experts". Oh, how much money I could have saved if I would not have tried to fix it myself, but had enlisted professional expertise from the get-go!

No matter how long we have had a relationship with God, we tend to try to work out our difficulties on our own before asking for God's help. Yes, we may pray at the outset but then rush ahead and fail to wait on God to do His "behind the scenes stuff". Trusting Him to do His part is nothing more or less than faith. Don't forget--when we work our way through situations we never have to do it alone.

Proverbs 3: 5 (MSG) "Trust God from the bottom of your heart; don't try to figure out everything on your own."

44
"JUST AROUND THE CORNER"

When I was a young boy, (just a few short years ago), I owned a squirt gun with a flexible barrel which allowed me to squirt around a corner at my "play enemy". Although not too accurate, I still had fun with this innovative toy.

We are finite people with limited knowledge. Fact is we really don't know what's around the corner. If we did, we might want to turn and run. Usually we think about negative things around the next turn. We think of disaster or bad news or even getting hit in the face by some saboteur.

Truth is-- there are often great and wonderful things just around the corner. However, you may never encounter them if you're not expecting them. God has tremendous plans for each of us, but we must keep on moving around the corners of our life until He decides the time is right. When it's time, they will refresh us. Meantime, stay on His side.

1 Cor. 2: 9 (MSG) "No one's ever seen or heard anything like this, never so much as imagined anything quite like it—what God has arranged for those who love him."

45
"IT'S A NEW YEAR!"

The author of much of the New Testament, Paul, tells us to "forget all the things which are behind". If he were living and writing today, I believe he'd say "get...over it".

All of us have things to "get over", especially "stuff" from the previous year. Whether good or bad, it's history now and time to "move on". We cannot go back and change anything--we must look ahead and forget the past.

By getting over it, we are in no way suggesting forgetting blessings and good things of the past. It's always beneficial to remember happy times, special occasions and significant accomplishments. However, the excess baggage of disappointments, heartaches and unrealized expectations need to be deleted from our memory banks. Of course we can recall them, but choose not to. Forgetting what is behind is not an easy assignment--never has been.

Consider the following suggestions:

1. We must want to "get over it". It all begins with our will. So much can be done when we really want to make it happen.

2. We must try to "get over it". Often, our "trying" is only talk and never materializes. We relegate ourselves to wishful

thinking which helps us temporarily escape but does not solve our situation.

3. We need an action plan. What steps will we take to get over our past? These steps need to be written so as to allow for referral and reminder.

4. Accountability is key--inform someone of your game plan and ask them to monitor you in your speech, decisions and associations. Be sure to pick someone who loves you enough to confront you.

A new year is in progress. It's OK to move forward and make it count. Oh yes, be patient with yourself.

Phil. 3: 13 (NLT) No, dear brothers and sisters, I have not achieved it, but I focus on this one thing: Forgetting the past and looking forward to what lies ahead...

46
"THE BEST"

I recall, growing up around my grandparents' home, being exposed to the Sears and Roebuck catalog. It was our "dream book" as we daily scanned all the stuff money could buy. Many products were available in three different grades-Good, Better, and Best. The cost escalated as the assigned quality of the item improved. One would be quite impressed with a "good" refrigerator until you read about a "better" one. Of course, the "best" one was always pictured which made it more enticing. You always felt like you were settling for second best if you did not select the "best" category.

Our choices in life are not much different. There are many good things we can choose to do or participate in; the options we have due to technology and resources are almost unlimited. Yet, choosing the "best" things is not always easy. We definitely need God's help to make right decisions.

Mediocrity has invaded our society at many levels. The pursuit of excellence is talked about but practiced less. Once-held values of doing a job right or standing behind a product unconditionally have basically disappeared. So, we tend to live in the "good" and "better" and even "improved" but seldom in the "best".

As those who name the name of Christ we are compelled to always strive for the Best-anything less is simply not biblical.

Matthew 22: 37 (MSG) Jesus said, "'Love the Lord your God with all your passion and prayer and intelligence.' This is the most important, the first on any list.

47
"HAPPY HOUR"

I was having lunch in a restaurant one day which had a sign over the main entrance announcing Happy Hour from 4-6 PM. This term, in our culture, has come to mean a time of drinking and socializing with friends following work and prior to dinner or other evening activities. While I do not participate in this kind of celebrating, it made me ask myself, "When is my happy hour?"

We all need a daily time to not only unwind and relax but to be genuinely happy. This is not to suggest we should be unhappy the rest of the day but simply to make room in our schedules to purposely have fun and recreate. Indeed, our "happy hour" does not need to be limited to 60 minutes, but one hour is certainly better than no time at all.

Happiness is a choice; therefore, we can decide to enjoy our life and our family and friends or to endure them. God did not put us here on earth to be miserable and sad. However, without planning to do things which bring us joy we tend to work too hard and pass up the "fun moments". Waiting till vacation time or the "weekend" is no substitute for the day by day deliberate scheduling of happy hour. Without such a plan we grow old too quick and die too young.

You may have to make your happy hour flexible each day to fit your "must do" tasks; but, do whatever you have to do to celebrate your God-given life by observing Happy Hour. Everyone around you will be glad you did!

Dt. 12:12 (MSG) You must celebrate there in the presence of the Lord your God with your sons and daughters...

48
"GOOD DAY"

We constantly make value judgments about nearly everything in life. Things are perceived as "good" or "bad" according to how they affect us. Our preferences are developed at an early age, and then we tend to spend the rest of lives trying to justify them or overcome them. For example, there was a time in my life when I did not like pizza. You see, pizza, as we know it today, was not a part of society then, at least in my community. When one wanted pizza the solution was to make your own Chef-Boy- R- Dee- do it yourself mix. The first ones I tried left much to be desired. I have long since become victorious over this eating malady.

Many sincere people do not understand what's good about Good Friday. To them it seems like a terrible thing that could happen to anyone, let alone the Son of God. To commemorate a day in which Roman capital punishment was executed on a "religious leader" is really morbid and politically incorrect. But, to one who truly believes and personally accepts the love and forgiveness of the man on the middle cross, it is a good Friday. In fact, it makes every day "good" for we know the story does not end on Friday.

It's good because it's PERSONAL-we understand He died not only for the world but especially for US.

It's good because it's POSITIVE-for the believer the cross is a PLUS sign.

It's good because it's PLENTIFUL-He died for WHOEVER will believe and receive Him as Savior.

It's good because it's POWERFUL-Christ Himself paid for our salvation.

Now, that's GOOD NEWS!

I Cor. 1: 18 (MSG) The Message that points to Christ on the Cross seems like sheer silliness to those hell bent on destruction, but for those on the way of salvation it makes perfect sense.

49
"TAKE IT TO THE NEXT LEVEL"

Both "experts" and life tell us that we either move ahead or slide backwards. There really is no room to stand still in our ever-changing world. We sometimes think we'd like for things to stay the same; fortunately, there are times for coasting and inactivity. But reality strongly suggests that life moves ahead with or without us.

Have you ever moved away from someplace and then revisited your former community expecting everything and everyone to be the same? It is quite a jolt to realize that life went on and you were not a part of it. The lesson is we can never go back but only forward.

It's in vogue today to talk 'bout "taking it to the next level", whether it be in sports or business, the principles are still the same. It will require us to stop doing some things and start doing others. We are usually very good at adding things to our life but often do a poor job of subtracting "stuff" from our agenda. Our lives get very complicated and full because we fail to do the math.

Curly, the crusty old cowboy in the movie City Slickers, reminded his tenderfoot guests that life is about ONE THING. When you find that one thing you can really live. Taking our lives to the next level necessitates that we simplify and focus our priorities. No person or institution can "do it all". Today's modern spacecraft cannot really take off until it jettisons the cumbersome fuel tanks. When that happens, astronauts are propelled to a new level of space and possibilities.

The Apostle Paul practiced Next Level Living. He said in one of his letters that we are to "forget those things which are behind". In other words, get rid of it because the next level has a baggage limit. Count your luggage-discard the irrelevant and move on up!

Phil. 3: 13 (NLT) No, dear brothers and sisters, I have not achieved it,[a] but I focus on this one thing: Forgetting the past and looking forward to what lies ahead,

50
"IMPATIENCE CAN DERAIL YOU"

I was on my way to my church to prepare for the service when I encountered a train blocking my road. It was raining quite hard, but the train seemed to be moving along at a consistent speed. Drivers in front of me began to turn around till I found myself at the front of the line. Through the splattering raindrops hitting my windshield I noticed the train slowing down; then, it stopped! I was already late to be at my destination and now this! Would it stay stopped for a long time? Would it begin backing up? Should I turn around and seek an alternate route?

During all this time, I decided to count the cars just to help the time pass. As each long coal car rolled past me I added it and noticed its markings. This allowed me to stop checking my watch and focus on my current situation.

Passive personalities have an easier time watching "things pass by" than active people. Being one who is active my patience quotient is not as high as it should be. Here are some things I'm learning from the train:

1. The likelihood of experiencing delay is in direct proportion to how late you're running.

2. By counting, I entered into the moment which relaxed me rather than continuing to fret.

3. My patience was not so great, but it did outlast those in front of me, which paid off.

4. Even when the train stopped halfway through, I was sufficiently calm to wait for it to move again; after all, I had not finished counting.

5. Life has a way of "training" us to be patient. The question is will we learn the lesson?

Don't be derailed by your impatience today--look for ways to enjoy the moment!

Ps. 40:1 (NLT) I waited patiently for the Lord to help me, and he turned to me and heard my cry.

51
"YOU ARE BEING QUOTED"

Being a public speaker, I am sometimes quoted by others, even kids. A little girl in my church heard me speak about the family. One of my lines was "Parents, be sure to listen to your children." Later in the week, an issue came up in the home of this same sweet girl, in which she instructed her parent s to listen to her cause the pastor said to.

She is to be commended for listening; but, it made me stop and think: how many people do listen to us each day and quote us in some way? They may not quote us directly or correctly, but they are being influenced by what we say. As moms and dads in the home, as supervisors at work, as leaders in our church etc., mark it down, someone, somewhere, is quoting you.

This can be a disturbing thought if we really think about it. Our words have more power than we realize. We can encourage and elevate others; we can also discourage and deflate people by even our tone of voice or facial expression.

It's probably a good rule that if you have nothing good to say then don't say anything. This will definitely reduce the probability of being misquoted.

Ps. 19:14 (NLT) May the words of my mouth and the meditation of my heart be pleasing to you, O Lord, my rock and my redeemer.

52
"I UNDERSTAND"

One of my good friend's, who is now in heaven, had a phrase he said quite regularly, "I understand". The effect of this statement upon the listener is most profound. It says, "I'm with you" or "I know where you're coming from" or "I'm hearing you without judgment."

In our critical world where misunderstanding abounds, it is extremely comforting to hear that someone does understand or, at the very least, is attempting to understand. To be understood is so therapeutic, releasing tension in us built up by the daily pressures we face. When "I understand" is said to us we feel loved, our self-concept is elevated and our person hood is affirmed.

All of us want to be understood. Even more important, each of us can be more understanding. May I encourage you to join me in practicing these healing words with your kids, spouse, friends and even strangers. They will go a long way in reducing problems and making life more pleasurable.

By the way, one of the many wonderful characteristics of the greatest teacher of all times, Jesus, is the fact He does understand- now, that's good news!

2 Tim. 2:7 (NLT) Think about what I am saying. The Lord will help you understand all these things.

53
"THANK YOU, THANK YOU, THANK YOU"

I was forced to buy a sweeper since our "good" vacuum had a blown motor. We had company coming, my Mom and Step-Dad, and so clean the house must be. Upon entering Wall-Mart, I passed the cash registers and picked up a pack of AAA batteries on my way to the sweeper aisle. As I started to inspect the various cleaning devices, I inadvertently placed the batteries in my pocket while moving some boxes, trying to find the "best deal". Later in the day, as I emptied my pockets, the forgotten batteries appeared. I was embarrassed and upset at myself for being so forgetful. However, I quickly forgave myself, realizing it was just a mistake, and decided to return the batteries and pay for them as soon as possible.

Monday came and I planned to return the batteries then. But, I had to go out of town to pick up my daughter at the airport so more delay. On the trip to the airport, I entertained these thoughts:

1. Look for another Wall-Mart and return them there since I have another item that needs to be returned. This sounded plausible, would be good use of time; but, it carried diminished, restitution impact.

2. Skip returning batteries altogether; after all, I had given "wally world" enough business over the years to merit a few, measly batteries. This option was summarily dismissed since it was WRONG, and I knew it.

3. Go back where you accidently took them and make it right.

At the courtesy desk, on Tues. morning, I waited as another customer made his return. I stepped up and presented my "return item" and received the proper credit. Even as this first item was being handled I still was plagued with thoughts of simply taking the batteries(concealed in a bag) and just going through a checkout line and paying for them as though I had just selected them.(no one would know) Finally the courteous customer service girl said "is there anything else?" I said "yes, there is" and proceeded to explain how I had taken the batteries by mistake and now wanted to pay for them. As she scanned the bar code she looked at me incredulously and said "thank-you" three times. When she handed me my change I said, "I wouldn't want to miss heaven over $3.56." Neither do you.

Luke 8:17 (MSG) We're not hiding things; we're bringing everything out into the open.

54
"DON'T COMPLAIN ABOUT WHAT YOU PERMIT"

We live in a world where many things are simply out of our control. We watch in utter helplessness as a crazed gunman kills and maims people in and wonder: what is happening to our world?

This same world confronts us with many daily choices. According to how or what we choose greatly determines our future. Faulty decisions can be corrected but often are allowed to go on and on, year after year, as we "endure" and "carry on". We excuse ourselves by rationalizing that it doesn't hurt too much, or it will probably get better "someday". Reality is it usually does not improve and often deteriorates.

This is graphically illustrated by the visitor who goes to a very rural home in the hills of Tennessee. As this visitor is being shown around the house, he notices an old hound dog lying on the front porch. Every few minutes the dog raises up a little and moans. Finally, the visitor has to know what's wrong with the dog, so he asks the owner, "what's the matter with your dog?" The man of the house replies, "Ah, that's old Butch! See, he's lying on a nail in the floor and every now and then he rises up a little to get some relief."

The visitor inquires further. "Why doesn't Butch just move to a new spot?" The owner says, "I guess he doesn't hurt bad enough to move."

We laugh at "old Butch" for his lack of ambition and complacency. But, we are not much better when we continue to complain about things in our life which are under our control and yet permit them to continue as though we're impotent to change. If it's in your power to improve your situation, then God, your family, friends and co-workers have a legitimate right to expect you to do so.

Next time you hear yourself complaining about something, remove the "nail of discontent" (change the situation) or remain silent. Your life will immediately improve, and those close to you will be grateful.

Ps. 142:1-2 (MSG) I cry out loudly to God, loudly I plead with God for mercy. I spill out all my complaints before him, and spell out my troubles in detail:

55
"LESSONS FROM THE BEACH"

My wife and I love to vacation on the Oregon coast. Those of you who have been there know how incredibly beautiful it is. Even though the beaches in the Northwest are different than in other parts of the country, they still have the same basic characteristics of other beaches which attract millions all year long.

While sitting on the sand, leaning up against a giant driftwood log, I had many impressions and thoughts--here are some:

1. The incessant waves remind us that time moves on. No matter what else happens the waves just keep on comin'. So it is with our lives-time moves on regardless of the interruptions. The consistent pattern of the waves and the tides denote a rhythm that only a Divine Creator could have imagined and implemented.

2. Some of the greatest sculptures have originated on the beach in the form of castles and moats, sand angels etc. These creations bring together families and, sometimes, even strangers to make them. But they too soon disappear as the waters once again climb the shoreline.

We recognize the parallel in our own lives as our best laid plans and work often disappear without a trace and we have nothing to show. Life is fleeting, at best, and we learn to enjoy the "now" rather than always delay fun.

3. Construction of a new bridge was taking place a few yards from us and yet was not a disturbance due to the roar of the surf. As long as we faced the ocean the sound of water rushing toward land served as an audible barrier which enhanced the scenery. As we go through life it is important to be facing the right direction; otherwise, the clanging noises of this world will rob us of peace and rest.

4. Finally, a day at the beach is definitely a gift from Almighty God. The complexities   of nature all come together just to make our day brighter. You have to love a God who blesses His children with such extravagance.

ECC. 7:13 (MSG) Take a good look at God's work. Who could simplify and reduce Creation's curves and angles to a plain straight line?

56
"TWO MINUTE WARNING"

I went to a high school football game that had no scoring until the fourth quarter. The visiting team made a couple of touchdowns which seemed to wake up the home team. Unfortunately, many of the fans left early and missed the most exciting action of the last two minutes. That's when the home team got serious and "almost" beat their opponent had time not expired. They played with a sense of mission and effectiveness that was not evident in the previous minutes.

Why is it that we do not play the game of life more effectively? That we often wait too late before we begin to focus our efforts towards winning rather than losing? We do well defensively and yet fail to put points on the board which is how the game is won.

Consider what would happen if you began your "two minute drill" earlier in life; to play with passion and with the firm belief that you've been placed here on earth not for the purpose of playing it safe but for carrying the ball over the goal line. Your Creator made you with built-in destiny. He expects you and me to "play all out" until the game is over. Oh yes, the two minute warning is silent.

James 4: 14 (NLT) "How do you know what your life will be like tomorrow? Your life is like the morning fog—it's here a little while, then it's gone."

57
"IN 5 SECONDS EVERYTHING CHANGED"

When Mother Earth shakes, it often results in the deaths of 100's of innocent people. We are saddened when we see such human suffering, especially of this magnitude.

As I watched one of the newscasts, a lady from Taiwan was being interviewed. She said "In five seconds everything's changed". Many 1000's of lives will never be the same-many will be no more. It's a real tragedy, and we pray for the families of the victims.

So much can change "our world" in a short amount of time. That phone call in the middle of the night which can announce the joyful birth of a new baby or inform us of an accident or loss of a loved one. Our priorities sort out very quickly, almost automatically, as we focus on the current crisis. Things we thought were so important disappear from our schedule as we devote our energy, money and time to the matter at hand.

Long-range planning is vital and necessary to our everyday lives. But, there is the fine balance of enjoying the "here and now"; to not miss the journey of life while we strive to reach our goals and destinations.

For sure, we will have our "five second" experiences and, when we do, we'll be so glad we took the time for that extra hug or phone call or quality time with our family and friends.

Ps. 77: 18 (NLT) "Your thunder roared from the whirlwind; the lightning lit up the world! The earth trembled and shook."

58
"SOME YOU LOSE, SOME YOU WIN AND SOME ARE CALLED ON ACCOUNT OF RAIN"

A good friend told me about one of his Grandpa's pithy sayings: "some you lose, some you win and some are called on account of rain". Besides being real funny, there is a lot of truth in this statement.

First, there are just some things in life that we all lose. We don't plan to lose necessarily, but it's simply inevitable. If we live long enough, we'll not only lose games and promotions but also critical items, like our hearing or even memory. Losing is never fun, no matter how "saintly" we might be. Life has its surprises, and many we'd like to avoid.

Thankfully, we do "win some". In fact, proper planning and attention to detail can often increase our wins. Even if we're self-effacing by temperament, it's still nice to have things go right, to achieve our goals and see our families excel. Many times God's Grace steps in and brings good things our way, even when we do nothing to deserve it. The only appropriate response is to be grateful to Him and to renew our loyalty to His leadership.

The third area is uncertain and unpredictable. We do not know what the outcome will be-it's not in our hands to control or in our power to influence. Certainly the weather falls in this category-many lives have been drastically altered by the forces of nature.

Human relationships also tend to fall in this division as free will is executed with the possibility of making wrong decisions. Sometimes, our decisions can terminate the game, and we're unable to have a make- up game. It is in this very arena of life that we most often live-how vital it is for us to be personally connected to the Eternal Umpire.

Ps. 116: 5 NLT " How kind the Lord is! How good he is! So merciful, this God of ours!"

59
"SEEING THROUGH THE GIANTS"

One day, as I drove to my home, I found myself following a garbage truck. Thankfully, my windows were up, but the smell was stronger. Just before the truck went one way and I another, I noticed the name GOLIATH on the top part of the back of the truck. Even more curious was the fact that the word GOLIATH also appeared further into the truck. I discovered the outer letters were cut outs, and so as the sun shone through, the name was reproduced in shadow form.

As we know, Goliath was a giant who opposed David and lost. He was quite formidable and should have easily defeated the little shepherd boy, but such was not the case. Through eyes of faith David launched his head-seeking missile, and the rest is history.

All of us have giants of one kind or another. They are usually intimidating and can cause us to want to run. However, upon closer examination, many of our "giants" are hollow-their "bark is worse than their bite". They are giants in name only with no real substance.

We must continually look beyond our "giants", and see how gigantic God really is. It's a great way to live!

1 Samuel 17: 50 NLT "So David triumphed over the Philistine with only a sling and a stone, for he had no sword."

60
"BEING WINSOME"

Webster defines WINSOME, a term we do not use much today, as "generally pleasing and engaging often because of a childlike charm and innocence". When we speak of someone with a winsome attitude we are complimenting them.

In today's world, "attitudes" have become a focal point of judging people and institutions. In other words, we characterize others by saying they are "positive" or "she has an attitude", meaning she is perceived as uncooperative, selfish or even belligerent. Companies are also depicted by their attitude towards technology or customers or quality.

In order for each of us to become more "winsome", I believe we have to begin "winning some" of life's challenges and as we do, focus on our wins and not our losses. All of us win more than we think, but we've been programmed to highlight how many we missed rather than accentuate how many we got right. Certainly this is not easy to do, but oh so necessary if we're to be productive and a good influence on anybody.

You may be thinking, "How do I start winning? It seems like my successes are buried by my continual problems." Well, don't feel like the "lone Ranger". You're not the only one in the battle-people all around you are struggling, even the ones who look like they "have it together". Just like we keep our bodies going with medicines, exercise and proper diets, we must also feed our minds and souls in a healthy manner. Consider these basic suggestions as you become more winsome:

1. Make sure your vertical relationship with God is current.

2 Hang out with the most positive people you can find-it will rub off.

3. Reprogramming your mind is vital and will require deliberate reduction of negative input along with increased doses of wholesome material.

4. Do something to help someone else!

People want to be with people who are winners. Having more friends is a definite blessing of becoming a "winning" person. You have everything to win and nothing to lose-GO FOR IT!

Luke 10: 27 MSG "That you love the Lord your God with all your passion and prayer and muscle and intelligence—and that you love your neighbor as well as you do yourself."

61
"AUTO PILOT"

We live in an automated world, at least here in North America. Time-energy saving devices are all around us. Most are great inventions, and yet our health tends to suffer while we are tempted to "veg" out and watch others exercise.

So many things in our society require very little thinking since they are pre-programmed to perform a service for us. They're great as long as they work, but occasionally something goes wrong. The late great golfer Payne Stewart and his fellow travelers were enjoying the luxury of auto pilot until the malfunction. While others searched the skies to find them, they simply continued flying straight for hours.

As we reflect on this terrible tragedy, consider with me the following:

1. In the daily routines of life, like travelling in a car, it is so easy to go along and not even be aware of where you are or what's happening all around you. With our on board computers, navigational systems, even familiarity with our route, we often find ourselves kind of on "auto", not remembering how we got to our destination.

2. Air Force pilots have told us the plane was flying perfectly straight. From all outward appearances, except the frost on

the windows, everything seemed to be OK. We too fly through life, and those around us usually do not detect any problems we may be experiencing. You see, we're on auto pilot-we know the drill, when to smile, what to say, how to deflect any investigation when all the while we may be "dead inside". Our emotional and spiritual oxygen has escaped and yet we seem to be unable to signal for help as others "fly by". And so, we fly on until we run out of fuel.

God has a better flight plan for our lives. He wants to be your pilot with you as the co-pilot. He never fails; no matter how high or low we get. All one must do is give Him the controls of your life and follow the Christian Flight Path. Don't forget to check in with your air traffic controllers (family, friends, a counselor, pastor, etc.) to update you on your location and progress. You don't have to "go it alone".

Ps. 31: 3-5 MSG You're my cave to hide in, my cliff to climb. Be my safe leader, be my true mountain guide. Free me from hidden traps; I want to hide in you. I've put my life in your hands. You won't drop me, you'll never let me down.

62
"A RETURN LAUGH"

One of my daughters shared with me a phrase that caught my attention- "a return laugh". She explained that it meant something funny out of the past that, when you think of it again, makes you laugh some more.

Humor is one of the greatest healers in our world. In fact, some forms of therapy prescribe laughing as a way to treat one's ailments, even life-threatening diseases. A wise man, inspired by God, once wrote "A happy heart makes the face cheerful...". It does bring a smile to our countenance when we recall a good, wholesome laugh that we shared with others.

We need to practice the art of return laughs, because there are many things which come along that are not funny. In fact, sometimes we go through days and weeks with a lot of negative stress and laughs become very scarce. If one is experiencing physical or emotional pain, it is simply difficult to appreciate humor or respond positively toward it. Therefore, it is helpful to have a "reserve" to draw from during the "down times".

Today is Thanksgiving Eve. I have SO much to be grateful for in my life. One of my top 5 is the ability to laugh, even when I don't feel like it. For sure, it's not always spontaneous but

must be primed by those who are closest to me.
Occasionally, out of nowhere, I am divinely touched and
alerted to the lighter side of a situation and for that I
unashamedly give praise to the God.

Ecc. 3: 4 MSG "A right time to cry and another to laugh, …"

63
"SEEING CLEARLY"

I lived on planet Earth for many years without the assistance of glasses. Finally, due to the persistence of my loving wife, I went to the eye doctor and discovered I not only needed glasses but bifocals too.

One day I got up early to take my son back to college. I grabbed my glasses from off the night stand and proceeded to get ready to leave my house. I noticed that my eyesight was blurry, so I cleaned my lenses. It was like I could see so much better without them. I had just put some drops in my eyes, so I thought it was a temporary situation. Since my sight was so greatly improved without the glasses the idea crossed my mind that God had healed me as I slept.

After starting my car I decided to discard the glasses for they were doing me absolutely no good. I opened my case and found a second pair of glasses-MINE! I had been wearing my wife's glasses by mistake.

Well, our family and friends had a big laugh over this one. It was an easy mistake to make yet it produced major complications. Trying to see through another person's prescription does not work--one size does not fit all.

When we see incorrectly, no matter what the reason, it distorts all of life and can lead to serious misjudgments about ourselves and others. Many go too long without prescription becoming blinder each day as they adjust to convoluted rather than corrected sight. Like me, they don't realize what things are supposed to look like since they have been viewing them wrongly for many years.

I'm grateful for both physical and spiritual sight. The former is important-the latter is essential.

"I once was lost but now I'm found; Twas blind, but now I see"

64
"THE POWER OF WAITING"

Most of us do not enjoy waiting; yet, we live in a world which provides unlimited opportunities to wait. We find ourselves being forced to wait in traffic, at the doctor's office, for an important phone call, for a decision--you name it. Waiting time seems to be "wasted time", which it can be if we allow it. Like so many things in life, we must use it to our advantage rather than our disadvantage.

Experience proves to us over and over that waiting has real power, although we're often slow to learn or accept the teaching. Many of our challenges simply fade away or get bumped by new problems if we wait long enough. It is in the waiting times that we can gain wisdom and insight. You may recall adults telling you to "just wait" and, being a kid, it made no sense at all to WAIT. But, upon more mature consideration, waiting gives time to develop a better strategy, to find more suitable solutions, etc.

Scripture instructs us that waiting on God can be renewing; give us new perspective, energy and drive. Like in auto racing, pit stops are vital to winning. Without them, it does not matter how fast we go-we will not go the distance. Likewise, the wait-stops are empowering if we allow them to be. AMEN!

IS 40:31 MSG But those who wait upon God get fresh strength. They spread their wings and soar like eagles, they run and don't get tired, they walk and don't lag behind.

65
"YOU'RE NOT THE ONLY ONE WHO'S UNDER PRESSURE"

My wife and I watched part of a TV show where a little girl, who is the daughter of the lady judge, gets upset at her mom. When the mother tries to talk to her she says "you're not the only one who's under pressure". It kinda hit her mom as a "wake up" call. It hit me with the same impression.

Christmas time is a stressful time to say the least. You have your regular monthly schedule, and then add to it extra parties, financial pressures, decorating, entertaining, travel, in-laws, etc. You have the makings for a near-collapse. In fact, many do check out as suicide rates soar during the holidays.

When we're stressed we tend to become so self-focused that we are oblivious to others or our impact on them. We just want to accomplish our "TO DO" list as quickly as possible. In this pursuit our misunderstandings with others are usually intensified as they also are tackling their agendas. So, tension mounts and robs us of the joy of the season.

As we navigate through this month of "busyness", let's remember that everyone we meet is "under pressure", which means they may not be as loving and patient as in other months. Give them some space; some benefit of the doubt, and it will ease your stress--guaranteed!

Eph. 4:32 MSG "Make a clean break with all cutting, backbiting, profane talk. Be gentle with one another, sensitive. Forgive one another as quickly and thoroughly as God in Christ forgave you."

66
"BECOMING A PERSON OF EXCELLENCE"

A new year has dawned. Each of us has crossed over into a new year with all our plusses and minuses. As the inevitable New Year resolutions come and some go, one we should consider embracing is to become a person of excellence. This is not to disparage our past or to be unrealistic about our future but to explore and expand our God-given blessings to the max.

Now, none of us intend to be just mediocre or average. But, life has a way of compelling us to seek a comfort zone which can distract us from our dreams-we settle for less than best in order to "survive". Having a life has to be more than just surviving-it involves continual development of our potential which then becomes virtually limitless.

Understand, in order to move up, we must jettison unnecessary baggage. The author of much of the New Testament describes it as "forgetting those things which are behind". It's not that we lose our memory-it is that we choose to focus on today and tomorrow instead of yesterday. It will require conscious effort to do this since the future is unknown and potentially scary, whereas the past is known and, therefore, more comfortable.

Sometimes, we shy away from the idea of "excellence" thinking it to be unachievable. It is not perfection but rather striving to be OUR best, to improve in areas in which we have control. To be sure, this is not a quick fix but a journey, a mindset toward being all we can be. The good news is we don't have to be better than others to excel--just improve yourself.

Although there are no short cuts to excellence, there is a direct route. The greatest speaker who ever lived once said "set your heart on his kingdom and all these things will come to you as a matter of course." Matt. 6:33 Phillips

So don't worry, and don't keep saying, "What shall we eat, what shall we drink or what shall we wear?!" That is what pagans are always looking for; your Heavenly Father knows that you need them all. Set your heart on the kingdom and his goodness, and all these things will come to you as a matter of course.

67
"WRITE YOUR OWN REPORT"

I have a good minister friend who has taught me a lot about life. One day I said to him that I had heard great reports about the church he was pastoring." He replied, "You should; I'm writing them".

I've thought about his statement many times--it is so relevant to where we all live. We are drawn to people who are positive, even though we may not be ourselves. We want to be around people who are "successful", although it is not always easy to do so, especially if we are going through difficult times ourselves. Still, upbeat people attract and instill enthusiasm in all they encounter. The question is: "How can I be more positive?

The person we believe the most is our self. Therefore, it is vital that we communicate in a positive way about our own person, our job, our family and everything that pertains to us. In others words, self-talk is so important for we are constantly hearing our self. So if we say things which affirm and lift and inspire, then our own spirit is elevated. On the other hand, if we run our self down, verbalize or write out our shortcomings, then we deflate our mood and that of those around us.

There are some who feel it is disingenuous to say we're fine if we're not. However, the people who've interfaced with me whom I respect the most are those who have kept on smiling through the pain and have given little or no indication that anything was wrong. These are the ones who continually choose to speak or write a positive report. Consequently, their lives have not been lived in vain. They know that this world is only an opening act for the real life which is to come.

Phil 4: 8 MSG "Summing it all up, friends, I'd say you'll do best by filling your minds and meditating on things true, noble, reputable, authentic, compelling, gracious—the best, not the worst; the beautiful, not the ugly; things to praise, not things to curse. Put into practice what you learned from me, what you heard and saw and realized. Do that, and God, who makes everything work together, will work you into his most excellent harmonies."

68
"LIVING OFF CAMERA"

Much has been written and said about celebrities and how they act on and off camera. The argument is that while on camera their actions matter, but when off camera, behavior is personal and private and not to be scrutinized.

This dichotomy of character is inflicting great damage on our culture, for we innately know that this will not work. Even though most of us will never star in a movie, we do have our places in the spotlight like being in charge at work or a teacher in front of our class.

All of us have times and situations where we are being watched more carefully than at other times. However, it is in the "other times" where we spend most of our time. It's easy to let down and become too lax in our decorum. Our reputation can be seriously damaged in these "quiet moments" if we're not careful.

The line we hear today is "I can do or be whatever I want as long as I don't hurt anyone." On the surface it sounds good, but upon further reflection, it is a very shallow way to live. We do impact others whether we're aware of it or not. Often that impact is never shared with us directly but has a way of "catchin" up with us when we least expect it.

It pays to live well both privately and publicly, for our lives are being videoed by our Creator for playback someday. There is no cutting room floor-all will be seen.

Stay close to the Director-He's building you a home that's "out of this world".

Mark 4: 22 NLT "For everything that is hidden will eventually be brought into the open, and every secret will be brought to light."

69
"KEEP YOUR EYE ON THE DONUT"

A sign in a bakery shop window reads: "Remember, my friend, as you travel through life, whatever be your goal, keep your eye upon the donut and not upon the hole."

These words are as applicable to all of us. Each day we have many opportunities to apply this saying to our lives. We make a choice to focus on real substance or to lament about what use to be.

It's so easy to see "holes" that we tend to miss the donut, the obvious, what's real and measurable. We can get so caught up with that which has been subtracted, cut out, that we miss what is left which is the bigger piece of reality.

"Donut thinking" is positive thinking. It is concerned with making the most of what is, not what use to be. In our negative, skeptical, over-analyzed world, it takes genuine effort to see things clearly. Constant clarification is vital if one is to "major on the majors".

A great way to remain "donut focused" is to subscribe to objective truth. The best I know of which has stood the test of time and guided millions of people is the Bible. Our subjective thinking usually leads us away from THE TRUTH. Inevitably, it will point us toward the "unseen" rather than the "seen". Common sense living has always been rooted in God's Holy Word-now more than ever!

Ps 119: 105 NLT "Your word is a lamp to guide my feet and a light for my path."

70
"CALLER #4"

In this communication age, we spend an inordinate amount of time waiting to talk to someone "live" on the phone. I called a medical office one day and was told I was Caller # 4. Well, my first thought was that's better than caller # 5 and higher. From time to time, I was alerted that I now was caller # 3, 2, etc. When I got to #1, the system recycled me and we started the fun all over again.

There is an unbelievable volume of communication going on in our world, and much of it is with computers, message machines rather than with people. We talk to our family through E-mail or text messages. All of this allows us to "stay on the run" but does not foster good relationships. Consequently, we seem to talk less and less with others and become more isolated. Our identity is swallowed up in technical terminology -caller #.

God has a better plan-it's called Prayer. Available 24/7, and there is no waiting. Since this system operates by faith, we know our message is being heard and often being answered even while we speak. There are no disconnects unless we choose to terminate the call. Most of the answers we're looking for have already been recorded in a book we call the Bible.

Furthermore, they're timeless and very relevant to whatever we're facing. Good news-God knows our name. Ours is a priority call because we're one of His kids.

Jeremiah 33: 3 MSG   "Call to me and I will answer you. I'll tell you marvelous and wondrous things that you could never figure out on your own."

71
"PUT YOUR DANCIN' SHOES ON"

One Sunday night a wonderful choir came to our church. Their repertoire was superb with many of the numbers very upbeat. Indeed, we all have different tastes when it comes to music; however, I was impressed when one of my senior members said, prior to the concert, "I got my dancin' shoes on". Her statement was so uplifting and arrested my attention.

Even though much of the music was probably more contemporary than my friend was use to, she made an incredible statement denoting her attitude and disposition. She was saying: "I've come to enjoy this and enter into the experience rather than resist or just endure it." Consequently, she had a great time because she planned to.

We encounter experiences almost daily which challenge our preferences and disturb our comfort zone. We are free to boycott and avoid things we find objectionable, and so we should. But, there are many wholesome and inspiring experiences we spoil for others and even cheat ourselves of because we pre-judge and disdain without even giving them a try.

Life is made to enjoy, but most of us are living beneath our privileges. God does not want us miserable one more second. Lighten up and "put your dancin' shoes on!

Psalm 122:1 " I was glad when they said unto me, Let us go into the house of the LORD." KJV

72
"LIFE IS LIKE BASEBALL"

Yogi Berra, famed catcher for the New York Yankees, once said: "Life is like baseball; it's 95% mental, and the other half is physical." We laugh at Yogi's use of statistics, but, he's probably more accurate than we care to admit. We know, in our hearts, that the way we think is critical to anything we do in life. Yet, we often go ahead and live as though we can change our actions while ignoring our thinking.

Like baseball, life has its good and not so good innings. We go through slump times when we can't seem to connect with life's pitches. Sometimes, we strike out repeatedly and wonder what we're doing wrong. In the field, we can "bobble" the ball and make silly mistakes that allow our opponent to go ahead.

The antidote to all of this is to keep swingin' the bat, stay in the game and play through it. Don't forget, your number one fan is Jesus.

Phil. 3: 12-14 MSG "I'm not saying that I have this all together, that I have it made. But I am well on my way, reaching out for Christ, who has so wondrously reached out for me. Friends, don't get me wrong: By no means do I count myself an expert in all of this, but I've got my eye on the goal, where God is beckoning us onward—to Jesus. I'm off and running, and I'm not turning back."

73
"DON'T LET ANYONE EAT YOUR LUNCH"

We live in a world of "lunch eaters", which is to say there are many things that can happen to us that rob us of our dreams, our security and happiness.

 Many people lose their lunch early in life and go on for years, often a lifetime, suffering the consequences. For example, a Sun. School teacher accuses the wrong student of misbehavior and "throws him out of class". I heard of this happening to a 14 year old boy who never returned to the class or any church. Now he is a middle-aged adult, and the pain of that experience is still fresh in his mind-he continues to avoid churches because an unsympathetic teacher misjudged him. Even more tragic, no one stepped in to provide him a new lunch.

When our Creator made us He knew all the challenges we would encounter. Not only did He know, but He also experienced life on earth up close and personal. Many people and circumstances were trying to eat our Lord's lunch but were totally unsuccessful. He never forgot the love and protection of his Father, and neither should we.

Ps. 52: 8 NLT "But I am like an olive tree, thriving in the house of God. I will always trust in God's unfailing love."

74
"BE ONE"

I found myself talking to my daughter about being around nice people and what a blessing that is. As we talked, it occurred to me that I can choose to be one. That is, to be a nice person for others to be around.

A little girl was overheard praying this prayer: "God, please make all the bad people good and all the good people nice." That's powerful insight! It's so easy to get wrapped in our own challenges, schedules and patterns that we forget about others to the extent we can even come across rude and insensitive.

To be a nice person is not automatic. True, some are born with pleasing, easy-going personalities which helps them relationally. Others have to be more deliberate in demonstrating kindness and understanding.

"Being One" involves our attitude towards God, ourselves and others. Too often people leave one of the three major components out which leads to frustration and failure.

Having a proper vertical relationship is paramount to all other relationships. One's self concept is greatly enhanced by being clean before God. Being nice and getting along with others becomes much less difficult when you're at peace with your Maker and yourself.

2 Cor. 6: 6 NLT "We prove ourselves by our purity, our understanding, our patience, our kindness, by the Holy Spirit within us, and by our sin"

75
"JUST UNDER THE SURFACE"

We live in a world of first impressions; of quick judgments about things and people. The comic phrase of "what you see is what you get" has become more of an excuse than a reality. Often we perceive the idea of "just under the surface" in a negative way, as though one is hiding something or is being devious.

Experience tells us there is much potential "just under the surface". We know from the study of marine life that our oceans hold tremendous resources in terms of minerals, food and hydropower. Likewise, most people have great possibilities within them, but they've been covered up by a sinful lifestyle or by the inability to jettison a rough upbringing. Thus, the finer qualities have continued to be submerged rendering them ineffective and virtually useless.

There is a tendency to understand Christianity in terms of its retirement plan (heaven) or as a restrictive set of rules. True, the future for a BELIEVER is out of this world; but, more importantly, God's plan from the get-go has been to make our lives, here and now, productive and influential as we navigate through life's ever-changing waters.

Count on it-you will be tempted, even today, to rush to judgment about someone by how they look or act.

Remember, just under the surface lies great potential for good and for God. Giving others the benefit of the doubt will raise their opinion about you and that's God's plan.

Luke 6: 37-38 MSG Don't pick on people, jump on their failures, criticize their faults— unless, of course, you want the same treatment. Don't condemn those who are down; that hardness can boomerang. Be easy on people; you'll find life a lot easier. Give away your life; you'll find life given back, but not merely given back—given back with bonus and blessing. Giving, not getting, is the way. Generosity begets generosity."

ABOUT THE AUTHOR

Jim Marshall was born in Athens, Ohio. He is a graduate of Ohio Christian University and George Fox Seminary (WES). Jim spent 8 years singing with Gospel Quartets. As a Pastor he has served seven churches in Ohio, Indiana, Oregon, Georgia and Alberta, Canada. He also served as a missionary with World Gospel Mission in Kenya.

Jim and his wife Marg have been married for 38 years, they have four children.

CONTACT JIM

jamestmarshall@gmail.com

www.PastorJimMarshall.com

www.ingramcontent.com/pod-product-compliance
Lightning Source LLC
LaVergne TN
LVHW051103080426
835508LV00019B/2030